WHAT A DAY

By Pat Birtwistle

Illustrations by Bradley Moore
Original Cover Drawing by Antonio Montana Morales

Patnor Publishing

ACKNOWLEDGMENTS

A heartfelt thanks to Pat Nelson (my friend and research consultant) for her help and encouragement, Nick Sidoti for his enthusiasm, wealth of ideas and insights; Ann Marie Crocco for allowing the students in her school to pilot these novelettes, Angela Marcov who piloted these novelettes and showed such enthusiasm, and to Carole McGregor and Judy Metler for their editing skills. And a special thanks to Paul Dayboll, Linda Roote and Bradley Moore for their help with how to best get these books printed and for creating our website.

Above all, a very special thanks to Norm, my husband and best friend, for all his hard work in making these books become a reality.

WHAT A DAY

By Pat Birtwistle

Illustrations by Bradley Moore
Original Cover Drawing by Antonio Montana Morales

WHAT A DAY

CHAPTER 1

The Best Day Yet

"You can go to the lake, but do not think of going to that old house. You are still in trouble. You cannot get into too much trouble at the lake," said Nick's Mom. But she did not think of all the trouble the kids would get into before the sun set.

Lunch was packed and off they went to the lake. Bob was not with the kids at the swamp and the old house. So, as they were going, they were telling Bob about all the trouble they had been in.

"Did we get into TROUBLE!" said Dan. "I could not go out of the house. My dad was so mad!"

"Mom gave me lots of jobs to do," said Kim. "She was upset for days."

"My mom and dad went nuts," Nick said. "Mom kept crying and telling me what trouble we could have been in at the swamp. She was so upset, Dad had to take her out to help her get over it. She still thinks that we are little kids."

"You think that's bad!" said Beth. "You should have a Dad who is a cop. He went on and on and on!"

"Well, we will not get into trouble at the lake," Bob said. "We'll just have the best day yet!"

But, as the day went by, the kids would be in big trouble.

It was hot on the block, but it would be cool by the lake. The kids wanted to swim. Soon, they would be in the water. They planned a day with lots of fun and NO trouble. The sun was out and on the way, they made plans.

When they got to the lake, they just sat looking at the water as it came up on the sand. Then, they made a raft and Kim and Beth got on it as Bob and Dan pushed it out into the lake.

They got the raft to a big rock and pushed the raft onto it. The kids liked to swim from the raft out there. Nick was the best one at swimming. He would get up on the raft and jump and do flips. The kids would see if they could do what he did. They were having a lot of fun.

At noon, the kids went back to have lunch on the sand. It was the best day yet!

"Look out there!" said Kim. "Way out there, it looks black. Do you think the rain will come this way?"

"The wind is not coming from that way," Bob said. "I think we will be OK! Let's get back to the raft."

So, they did.

"This is a trick I saw on TV." Nick said, as he jumped into the water.

The kids all did the trick and then got back up on the raft. That was when things went bad. Nick was running to jump into the water. Beth was just coming up onto the raft. Nick did not see her. As he jumped, Nick hit Beth and she fell back into the water. Nick came up, but Beth did not. All the kids jumped in to look for her. They could not see well. They could not see Beth at all. The water looked black, and the sky was getting blacker. It began to rain.

"Where are you, Beth?" Nick was thinking. "Come on! Where are you? I have to find you. You have to be OK!"

Bob came up out of the water. "What are we going to do?" he asked Kim as she came up.

"We will just have to stay down. We must find her. If we could just see down there, it would help. This water looks black. She cannot last down there. Let's go!" she said as she went down into the water.

CHAPTER 2

Beth's Trouble

Kim came up to rest. She could see Bob in the water to her left. Nick kept coming up and going back down into the water. Dan could not swim too well, so he had to stay by the raft when he came up. At last, when Bob came up. He yelled to Kim. "Here, get Nick and Dan over here. I think I see her!"

The kids all went to that spot. Bob had seen Beth in the mud. She lay still. She had hit a rock when she fell and had blacked out.

They pushed her up a little way. Then she would go back down. They could not get her up to the raft. Up they went, then back down. At last, they pushed her up to where the raft was.

Dan and Kim got up on the raft. Bob and Nick helped from the water. At last, they got her up on the raft. Her skin looked white and felt cool. The kids dragged Beth to the end of the raft. Kim pushed on Beth's ribs. It did not help. Kim pushed. Stopped. Pushed. Stopped. A little water came up. Kim kept pushing on Beth's ribs. At last, a lot of water came up.

"Did I kill her? I did not see her when I jumped!" Nick kept yelling.

"Nick, stop yelling. We will have to see what she is like when I get the water out," Kim said.

Beth's skin was still white. She just lay there. At last, Kim stopped pushing when Beth got rid of a lot of water. The kids all looked down at Beth. Nick was still saying, "Come on Beth! Come on Beth!"

Then, Beth looked up at Kim. Kim could not tell if Beth could see her or not. She rubbed Beth's hands and said, "Come on Beth. You can make it. Look at me."

"Will she be OK?" Bob asked.

"Do you think she will?" Nick asked Kim.

"I cannot tell," said Kim. "Her skin is so white, and she took in a lot of water. Rub her hands."

At last, Beth said softly, "I'm OK. I just want to rest a little."

The kids sat on the raft thinking of what trouble they would be in if Beth had not come to. It was hot, but the kids did not think of swimming. They just sat looking at the water. Dan was looking at something way out on the lake. It was coming to the raft.

"What is that thing way out there?" Bob asked. Dan had been looking at it too. "I can't tell what it is from here," he said.

All the kids but Beth got up to take a look. They could not tell what it was.

"There are lots of things out there," said Dan. "Let's stay here and see if the stuff comes this way." Beth got up to look, too. She fell back. She could not get up just yet. But, she did want to see what they were looking at.

Nick helped her sit up so she could see.

Lots of stuff was bobbing on the water. Some of it was bigger than the raft.

"I could swim out to find out what's there," Nick said. "I could swim out there with no trouble."

"No way!" all the kids said. "It is way out there and it's raining. It could get bad. Stay here!"

"We had all the trouble we want for one day," said Beth softly. "The stuff is coming this way. We will soon see what it is. Just stay here."

As the kids were looking at the stuff, Kim was thinking that yelling came from that way. "Did a cry come from out there?" she asked.

Now all the kids stopped.

"Help!"

The cry had come from the stuff out there on the lake.

CHAPTER 3

Will Nick Make It?

"What was that?" asked Kim.

"I think a cry for help came from out there," Bob said, as he looked out.

"That's it!" said Nick. "I am going out there. You stay here, and I'll be back."

He jumped into the water before the kids could stop him. Beth just sat on the raft. She wanted to stop him, but she could not.

"Nick, let's just stay here and see if we can help! If you swim out there, you may not get back," Dan was yelling at him.

But Nick kept swimming. He did not slow down. He wanted to do something. He kept thinking of what he did to Beth. Maybe he could make it up to her by seeing who had yelled for help. Maybe he could help them.

The rest of the kids can not swim well. If Nick gets into trouble, no one can help him. Nick soon gets way out by the stuff in the water. The kids can not see him too well. It now looks as if he is swimming to one thing. He is not looking at anything else in the water. He swims to one big thing. It looks bigger to Bob, Dan and Kim. What can he be looking for? Why does he just go to that one thing? Is that where the cry is coming from? Is he in trouble out there? The kids want him to come back to the raft, but he is not coming back.

"Should we get the raft out there?" asks Kim. "He is away out. He can get into big trouble out there by himself."

The rest of the kids could not swim well. If Nick got into trouble, no one could help him. Soon, Nick was way out by the stuff in the water. The kids could not see him too well. Now it looked as if he was swimming to one thing. He was not looking at things that were in the water. He was swimming to one big thing. It looked bigger to Bob, Dan and Kim. What could he be looking for? Why did he just go to that one? Was that where the cry came from? Was he in trouble out there? The kids wanted him to come back to the raft, but he was not coming back.

"Should we get the raft out there?" asked Kim. "He is away out. He could get into big trouble out there by himself."

"We cannot swim that well, and Beth is not up to it," Dan said. "We should stay here and see if Nick makes it back OK."

As Nick got out to the stuff in the water, he was looking for what could make that cry. He saw bits of this and that. He could not see too well. It was raining softly, and there was too much stuff in the water. A little way off, he could see what looked like a mast from a ship. He went to take a look. He wanted to rest, then get back to the kids on the raft.

He was swimming to the mast when something hit him from the left. This stopped him. He went down, came up, went down. He grabbed something and rested on it. After a bit, he went on his way. At last, he got to the mast. As he got to it, he could see a hand resting in the water. He could tell it was a man's hand. As he came up to the mast, he could see a man and a little girl.

Nick got up on the mast to see how they were. They just lay there. The man had a cut, and there was a lot of blood, but the girl looked OK. She was red from the sun.

She looked at him and asked, "Can you help my dad?"

Nick had to do something. Just then, water came up onto the mast. That made the mast tip and all three of them fell into the water.

"Not this!" Nick was thinking. "I do not think I can help them get out of the water."

Nick grabbed the little girl. He dragged her up to the mast, but she pushed him and went down to find her dad. Nick got her up and yelled at her. "You stay here! Do not get back into the water. I will get your Dad, if you stay on the mast. If you don't stay on the mast, he will die in the water. Stay here!"

"OK," she said, softly sobbing.

Nick went down into the black water. As he was going down, he was asking himself, "If I do find him down here, how will I get him up? It took all of us to get Beth up on the raft and this is a man, not a girl. I must find him. I wish I had help!"

CHAPTER 4

What To Do

"We cannot just sit here!" Dan said at last. "I cannot see Nick at all."

"Not one of us can swim all that way," said Bob. "Nick is the swimmer. Can you girls see him?"

The girls could not. The kids were all thinking that he would not come back.

"We have to do something," said Beth. "Can we get this raft out there to him?" She was up and looking out at the lake.

That was it! Bob jumped off the raft and pushed it. But the raft was stuck on a rock and he could not get it off! Dan went into the water, and the girls helped them. At last, the raft left the rock. Dan and Bob jumped back on. The kids lay on the raft. They could not get it to go out to where Nick was. The water kept pushing the raft back to land.

"We'll have to swim if we want to get out there," said Bob.

They went into the water and hung onto the raft. They made it go to where they had last seen Nick.

"I can't to this," Beth said. She still felt sick from being in the water.

"Let's do this," Bob said. "Kim and I will stay in the water and push the raft. When we want a rest, Dan, you and Beth can push. That way, it will not be as much trouble. Beth, do you think you can help?"

"I will be OK," said Beth. All the kids liked that plan. So that is what they did. No one had seen Nick. They kept looking at the spot where they had last seen him. When they all stopped to rest, Dan said to Beth, "Are you OK? You look as if you should rest."

The kids all had to rest. They got back on the raft.

"I'm OK," Beth said. "Nick is the one I'm thinking of. He has not been seen. I think he is in trouble."

The kids were thinking that too. They could not think of a way to get out there faster. Kim jumped back into the water. Bob jumped in too. They pushed the raft as best as they could. Dan jumped into the water, and they all pushed the raft. When they stopped to rest, Dan looked out at the stuff bobbing up and down on the lake.

"I think I can swim out there," Bob said, as he got back on the raft. "I can get out to Nick when I am rested."

Before the kids could stop him, he jumped into the water and was swimming out to Nick.

"Come back!" Kim yelled. "You will just get into trouble."

But Bob kept going. If no one could see Nick, it had to be bad. He felt that if he stayed with the raft, it could be the end of Nick. He swam faster. "I can do this! I can do this!" he kept thinking. "I must do this!"

When they saw what Bob was doing, the girls and Dan were in the water in a flash and pushing the raft as fast as they could. They had to stay with Bob. If he got into trouble, they wanted to be there to help him. He was not the best swimmer.

"Bob, you are soooo..." Dan was saying. He could not say what he wanted to. Water went over the raft, and the kids went down.

"How can this be?" Beth was thinking. "What are we going to do? Nick is not here to help. I am not well. Bob is way out there and cannot see that we are in trouble. Dan is not the best swimmer. I wish we had not come to the lake at all. What a day we've had. What are we going to do now?"

CHAPTER 5

What A Day

The water came over the kids, pushing them down. They had to get out of this mess so they swam to the raft. Kim grabbed Beth and helped her up onto the raft. Dan was kicking and bobbing up and down, so Kim helped him next. They rested a bit. They wanted to just lie on the raft and not get up at all. But they had to help Bob and Nick, so they went back to pushing the raft. At last, they got to the stuff in the water. They all got up on the raft. They could see no one. They yelled, "Bob, Nick. Where are you?"

They stopped yelling and looked all over. Things bobbed up and down on the water, but no one yelled back. The kids yelled, then stopped. Yelled, then stopped. Nick and Bob did not yell back.

"What are we going to do?" Kim asked. "There is so much stuff out here. If they are here we may not find them. What are we going to do?"

Bob had seen them and yelled, "I'm over here!" He swam to the raft. As he got up on the raft he said, "I'm here but I cannot see Nick. Let's stay cool. Think! Look for him! Yell!"

The kids did just that. Then they took a last look. They still could not see Nick. The girls were getting upset.

"We must stay cool and get help," said Dan.

"No!" Beth said. "We cannot go back. What if Nick is still out here and cannot yell for help?"

She still felt sick, but she did not let on. She wanted to go back too, but they all had to stay and find Nick.

"We should do as Dan said," Bob said. "There is too much stuff here and Nick has not yelled for help. We will not find him if we ....."

"Look - out there!" Kim yelled.

"Where?" asked Beth.

"There," said Kim. "See all that stuff and to the left is what looks like a mast."

The kids all saw the mast. Nick was on it and he was with a girl and a man. The kids all went into the water and pushed the raft to the mast. They could not think of why Nick did not yell back.

As they got to the mast, Nick did not say a thing. He looked odd. They could find out why, when they got back to land. Now, they must do all they could to get all of them back to land.

Beth and Kim helped the girl onto the raft. Then the kids got Nick on. The raft slid away. The kids pushed the raft up to the mast. The man lay still. Dan held the raft as Bob and the girl pushed the man from the mast onto the raft. The raft went down into the water, so Bob and Dan got off the raft and held onto the back and kicked. They were not going too fast so Kim got into the water and pushed as well. The little girl sat looking at her Dad. She had her hand in his.

At last they got to land. The girls stayed with the raft, Nick, the girl and her Dad. Bob and Dan ran for help.

When it was all over, the kids were in trouble and they could not go off the block. They did find out that the man got well. He and his little girl had come to the lake and were on this ship. They had hit a rock, and their ship had crashed. The man had put the little girl onto the mast, but then he had blacked out. If the kids had not been there to help, no one wanted to think of how that day would have ended for them.

Their folks kept asking if there was some way that they could stop the kids from getting into trouble! But, they could not find a way of stopping the kids. No one could think of a plan.

"How can you get into all this trouble?" Kim's mother asked. "This was to be a fun day at the lake and all you kids did was find trouble!

"Mommm, we were just having fun! We do not look for trouble. Do you think trouble just finds us?" asked Kim.

www.ingramcontent.com/pod-product-compliance
Lightning Source LLC
Chambersburg PA
CBHW060646030426
42337CB00018B/3477